Divine Providence and Human Freedom

Divine Providence and Human Freedom

OUR ROLE IN GOD'S PLAN

Dom Pius Mary Noonan, O.S.B.

CANA PRESS

Quotations from Holy Scripture
are taken from the Douay Rheims Version.

CANA PRESS © 2021

All rights reserved

No part of this book may be reproduced or transmitted, in any form or by any means, without permission.

For information, address:
PO Box 85
Colebrook,
Tasmania, 7027,
Australia

notredamemonastery.org

ISBN
978-0-6488688-8-0

Dedication

To Archbishop Julian,
Father in Christ,
Chosen Co-Worker of Divine Providence

Contents

Preface	1
1 Providence and God	5
2 Providence and its Co-Workers	17
3 Providence, Evil and Chance	36
4 Providence and Prayer	52
Conclusion—Providence and Hope	66
Appendix	69

Preface

*For those who love God,
all things work together unto good.*[1]

WITH THOSE FEW words the Apostle Saint Paul summarises one of the most consoling truths of our faith for those who believe, but one of the most challenging and even confronting for unbelievers. How often do we encounter people who are bitterly opposed to belief in God because of the bad things that have happened to them personally or to the world in general? St Paul's affirmation takes on directly and unabashedly these doubts and anxieties. At the same time he stimulates us and provokes our reflection. If you love God, he seems to say, all will turn out well for you in the end. Which is not to say that you will not have trials and suffering. But in the end all will be well.

What about those who love God and for whom things do not seem to turn out well at all? And those who certainly do not love God, or even believe in Him, and for whom everything seems to happen according to their wishes? Is it really possible to give a cogent answer to these questions?

The intention of this book is to tackle them with the light of the Gospel and the warmth of Christian charity. To do so, let me say from the very start that I am writing from the perspective of one who believes in God, in Jesus Christ, in all that

---

[1] Rm 8:28.

is authoritatively and definitively taught by the Holy Roman Catholic Church. I also hold firmly that human reason has the capacity to discern the truth. It is hoped that believers will find in these pages strength and encouragement in their life of faith, along with a number of answers to share with those who are not of our conviction. It is also hoped that the latter will be provoked and challenged to discuss the issues here raised, for they are among the most fundamental that every human being must face at some stage in life.

The providence of God contains many mysteries for the human intellect. I do not have the presumption to resolve these mysteries. I do, however, intend to demonstrate that, not only is the teaching of the Church on this point coherent, but also that it is really the only solution to the enigma of reality. Either there is a God who is guiding all things to their end, or there is nothing but despair. It is rigorously true that—to quote the title of a recent book by a prominent cardinal—it is "God or nothing".

I intend to first offer a number of reflections on the reality of Divine Providence. Indeed, reason itself shows us that there is a God who designed the universe and who therefore must guide its progress. After this, we shall turn to a consideration of what we learn through Divine Revelation as manifested in Sacred Scripture. A number of examples will be given here, affording us the opportunity to see, as it were, Providence in action in the concrete events of our lives.

However, as we contemplate the sovereign domain of God over all things, His absolute freedom to intervene at any moment to guide events and achieve His eternal plans, we cannot overlook the role which creatures play in bringing about the ultimate goal of the universe, namely the glorification of God and the salvation of souls. God provides for everything. Such is a clear teaching of Holy Scripture. And yet, angels and men are truly free to act on their own initiative. How can we explain that? Do the latter really play a role in the functioning of the universe, or are they not more like very sophisticated machines which the Creator uses, in the same way that men use computers to guide their vehicles?

This question, which in all truth has been agitated for millennia, lies at the very heart of man's reflections upon himself and his place in the world. Accepting or refusing to allow human beings to be real, efficient causes will determine the way in which one considers social relations in this life and eternal destiny in the next. In these pages, we will explore this question, taking as our guide the Divine Revelation itself as found in Holy Scripture and the teachings of the holy doctors, in particular that of St Thomas Aquinas, whose great synthesis has been formulated thanks to what he learned from the Bible and the Fathers of the Church.

In so doing, we inevitably run into the grave problem of evil in the world. No serious contribution to the question can be worthwhile without seeking to understand the place that evil can have in a universe which is substantially and fundamentally good. In the same way, the question of "chance" must be approached in such a way as to see its place in the loving oversight of an omnipotent God.

It will then be appropriate to address the specific question of the rational creature in a world which is under the care of a Divine Intellect, and see how Providence keeps watch over all things and leads them to their eternal destiny. These considerations will lead us to some of the most fascinating aspects of the spiritual life, in particular, to the role of human mediation and prayer in guiding the world to its ultimate destiny.

We are dealing here with one of the most difficult problems that has tormented the greatest philosophers. It is also one of the greatest mysteries of the Christian faith. As we approach it, we are reminded of the words of the prophet: *Seek not the things that are too high for thee, and search not into things above thy ability: but the things that God hath commanded thee, think on them always, and in many of His works be not curious.*[2] Should we not approach this subject with fear and trembling? Certainly. At the same time, the Angelic Doctor himself reminds us that even those who do have this holy fear of God are not forbidden from investigating divine realities. If their desire is to comprehend the incomprehensible, it is amiss and will fail, but if their desire is to know and submit their intellect to the truth, it can only be pleasing to God, for then it becomes *fides quaerens intellectum—faith that seeks to understand*, according to the famous expression of St Anselm of Canterbury. In this perspective, the fear of God helps the mind regulate itself on divine truth, submitting to it, and knowing when to accept in faith what it cannot fully understand. By proceeding in this way, a man is "investigating things which pertain to Divine Providence so that he may subject his intellect to divine truth, and not oppose divine truth which would be against the reverence for the fear of God".[3] A consummate model of this is found in Aquinas' saintly mentor, St Albert the Great, for whose feast day we are reminded that he was "great in subordinating human wisdom to divine faith".[4]

At the end of these pages, it is to be hoped that the reader will be renewed in love for the All-loving Hand of Divine Providence, and in zeal for cooperating with It.

---

[2] Sir 3:22.
[3] St Thomas Aquinas, *Commentary on the Book of Job*, ch. 9, lecture 4 (Translation by Brian Mulladay).
[4] "In humana sapientia divinae fidei subjicienda magnum effecisti" (*Missale Romanum 1962*, feast of St Albert, 15 November).

1
Providence and God

Thy providence governeth, O Father.[1]

IN THE VERY first article of the Apostles' Creed, all Christians profess: *I believe in God, the Father Almighty, Creator of Heaven and Earth*. Through these words, we profess that the universe exists only because it was brought into existence by a Supreme Being, Creator of all things, visible and invisible. This is what is referred to, in scholastic terms, as *creatio ex nihilo*—creation out of nothing. This means that before creation—inasmuch as we can speak of there being a time before time began— there was only God. God, by His own omnipotence, drew all things out of nothing. They did not exist before. They do now. They were created.

It is not the work of this book to develop this thought in detail. A word however might prove helpful to clarify just a little this first article of the creed, upon which all the others are based. After two centuries of Darwinian-based theories of a universe that would evolve on its own, there is much confusion in the air. I would simply like to say this: if it is possible to conceive of matter that always existed—St Thomas Aquinas is famous for having maintained that this is indeed possible—it is not possible to conceive of matter that exists *on its own*. This means that the human mind cannot really conceive of a purely material universe

---

[1] Wisdom 14:3.

with nothing else behind it. Why is this? Simply because we know from experience that no material object has within itself its own reason for existing; in other words, no material object can be its own origin, nor can it suffice to maintain itself in existence. Every material object is contingent on others. This means that all of them together are dependent on something or someone else who, of necessity, cannot be material, but has to be spiritual, that is to say, not include any matter whatsoever, for only something immaterial could ultimately be the cause of something that is material. This other being also has to have intelligence, for the very simple reason that there is intelligence in the world, and if there were no ultimate and supreme spiritual intelligence, no intelligence at all could possibly exist and the world as a whole would not be intelligible.

The fact of creation, then, is taken here as a given. If there were no Creator, there would be no creation. If there were no God, there would be nothing. "For without the Creator the creature would disappear".[2] But if there is creation, if there is a world, if there are things, then there is One who brought them into existence.

Going further, the bringing of things into existence by an immaterial, omnipotent God would seem of its very nature to imply more than just creation. For if God made things, it means that He has some reason for having done so, and therefore creation has what we call finality. What is that finality? What is that end? It can be none other than God Himself. Creation exists in order to allow other beings to share in the existence and love of God.

> "God, infinitely perfect and blessed in himself, in a plan of sheer goodness freely created man to make him

---

[2] Vatican Council II, Pastoral Constitution *Gaudium et Spes*, no. 36.

share in his own blessed life. For this reason, at every time and in every place, God draws close to man. He calls man to seek him, to know him, to love him with all his strength. He calls together all men, scattered and divided by sin, into the unity of his family, the Church. To accomplish this, when the fullness of time had come, God sent his Son as Redeemer and Saviour. In his Son and through him, he invites men to become, in the Holy Spirit, his adopted children and thus heirs of his blessed life".[3]

If God has created the universe for a specific end, then this would entail that He has some way of guiding it to that end, and this is precisely what we call providence. What do we mean when we speak of providence in God? Quite simply, we mean the plan according to which things are ordained to their end by the Divine Mind. The word *providence* and the word *prudence* have the same Latin root, namely *providere*, that is, literally, "to see ahead, to foresee", to project plans for the future. Someone who makes plans for the future is being provident; we can even say he is being providen*ce* for someone and for something. The etymology of the word, in particular the link between providence and prudence, shows the importance this latter virtue is going to have in determining what is truly providential. In other words, the choice of the right actions—which includes taking counsel and deliberating before deciding what is best as dictated by the virtue of prudence—is necessary in order to be provident.

If this is so, how can we say that God is provident, since He sees all things from His eternity and does not need the virtue of prudence in order to make the right decisions? First of all, as already stated, to speak of providence in God, is to speak of the plan according to which things are ordained towards their

---

[3] *Catechism of the Catholic Church*, 1.

end in the Divine Mind. Indeed, it belongs to prudence to order things towards their end, but in God Himself there can be nothing ordered towards an end, since He *is* the last end. Therefore this providence in God is ordered to other things, all things He has created.

Boethius put it this way: "Providence is the divine reason itself established in the highest ruler of all things, the reason which disposes all things that exist".[4] This foresight of God is precisely the way in which the creative wisdom manifests itself, and we see here an analogy with human prudence. Holy Scripture praises Divine Providence as the supreme authority over the world, who is full of solicitude for all creatures—especially for man—, for God uses the efficacious power of created things in order to realise His designs.[5]

The Church expresses God's providence in the following way: "By His providence God protects and governs all things which He has made, 'reaching mightily from one end of the earth to the other, and ordering all things well'.[6] For 'all are open and laid bare to His eyes',[7] even those things which are yet to come into existence through the free action of creatures".[8]

This teaching had already been expressed in poetic fashion by the holy man Job who describes in lively terms this absolute empire of God over the world:

"Behold, God is great, exceeding our knowledge:

---

[4] Boethius, *The Consolation of Philosophy*, IV, 6, translation by S. J. Tester, in LOEB, 1978, p. 359. This text is quoted by St Thomas Aquinas in *Summa Theologiae*, Ia, q. 22, a. 1.
[5] Cf. St John Paul II, *General Audience* 14 May 1986.
[6] Wisdom 8:1.
[7] Heb 4:13.
[8] First Vatican Council, Dogmatic Constitution *Dei Filius*, quoted in *Catechism of the Catholic Church*, 302.

the number of His years is inestimable. He lifteth up the drops of rain, and poureth out showers like floods: which flow from the clouds that cover all above. If He will spread out clouds as His tent, and lighten with His light from above, He shall cover also the ends of the sea. For by these He judgeth people, and giveth food to many mortals".[9]

In fact, the Old Testament portrays magnificently in numerous ways the far-reaching foresight of Divine Providence. One of the most astounding episodes revealing God's providence is that of the patriarch Joseph who was sold into slavery by his brothers. Years later, when they recognise him in the person of the ruler of Egypt, they are terrified. But their younger brother, whom they had thought forever gone, but is now lord of the land, says to them: "God sent me before, that you may be preserved upon the earth, and may have food to live. Not by your counsel was I sent hither, but by the will of God: who hath made me as it were a father to Pharao, and lord of his whole house, and governor in all the land of Egypt... Fear not: can we resist the will of God? You thought evil against me: but God turned it into good, that He might exalt me, as at present you see, and might save many people".[10] Through the short-sighted plans of wicked and ill-intentioned men, it is in reality Divine Providence that realises its own merciful designs over humanity.

Commenting on the verse of Job 5:13: "Who catcheth the wise in their craftiness, and disappointeth the counsel of the wicked", St Gregory the Great highlights in his *Moralia* how, in reference to the story of Joseph, the perverse motivations of

---

[9] Job 36:26-31.
[10] Gen 45:7-8; 50:19-20.

men can achieve exactly the opposite of their intentions, for the reason that they are guided by God. Crafty manoeuvres can be bent by the power of the Almighty, causing them too to execute the will of God even while they are labouring to thwart it. Foolish opposition to the divine ordinance is turned into cooperation with the very decree it refuses:

> "Joseph was sold by his brothers so that they wouldn't worship him, yet he was actually worshiped after he was sold. They ventured to do the crafty thing so that God's plan might be thwarted, but in trying to turn aside God's judgment, their resistance forwarded it. Where their crafty action had the object of altering God's will, there precisely they were forced to fulfill it. Just so, when God's plan is put aside, it is fulfilled. When human wisdom resists, it is caught. Joseph's brothers were afraid he might prevail over them; nevertheless, the avoiding of God's dispositions ends up by forwarding them. So human wisdom is tripped up by itself when it intends to resist God's will, and that act brings about its completion".[11]

David is another example of the amazing way in which Divine Providence looks after his servants. In his efforts to be rid of the young David, King Saul consents to give him the hand of his daughter in marriage, but he cunningly lays down a condition: David must bring him the foreskins of a hundred Philistines. Saul's intent is that David will easily be killed by the Philistines before he can achieve such a feat. In the end, David returns, not with a hundred foreskins, but with two hundred—an astounding exploit. This success had the

---

[11] St Gregory the Great, *Moral Reflections on the Book of Job*, Vol. 2, Book VI, XVIII, 29, translation by Brian Kerns, O.C.S.O., Liturgical Press 2015, pp. 56-57.

exact opposite effect intended by Saul: instead of being rid of David, he provided him with the opportunity for fame and popularity, paving his way to the throne. Saul's plan turned against him, because Divine Providence was watching over the young prophet and future king of Israel. "Saul was of course beaten by the net result of this deed of valor and caught by God's Providence in his wise plan. Where he thought he was taking the life of a successful soldier, he was actually adding to that soldier's honourable career".[12]

The Prophet Jonah can also be mentioned here. When he receives the command to go and preach to the corrupt people of Nineveh, instead of doing as he is told, he runs away, setting out in the exact opposite direction. A gigantic storm arises on the sea, the ship is in danger, the sailors cast lots to discover the cause of their misfortune, and the lot falls to Jonah, who is then thrown into the sea and swallowed by the whale. It is this irrational beast who spits him out on the shore of the very land God was sending him to. God, writes again St Gregory, "turns around for his own purpose and uses the very thing through which the man wanted to contradict him".[13]

In the New Testament, Our Saviour Himself, the new Moses, while promulgating the New Law on the Mount of the Beatitudes, assures us that nothing escapes the providence of God, not even the birds of the air and the lilies of the field. This is one of the best known texts of all Holy Scripture, and deserves an attentive reading here: "Behold the birds of the air, for they neither sow, nor do they reap, nor gather into barns: and your heavenly Father feedeth them. Are not you of much more value than they? ... Consider the lilies of the field, how they grow: they labour not, neither do they spin. But I say to

---

[12] St Gregory the Great, ibid., p. 57.
[13] St Gregory the Great, ibid., p. 58.

you, that not even Solomon in all his glory was arrayed as one of these". But the application to human beings is even more poignant: "And if the grass of the field, which is today, and tomorrow is cast into the oven, God doth so clothe: how much more you, O ye of little faith? Be not solicitous therefore, saying, What shall we eat: or what shall we drink, or wherewith shall we be clothed? For after all these things do the heathens seek. For your Father knoweth that you have need of all these things. Seek ye therefore first the kingdom of God, and his justice, and all these things shall be added unto you".[14] There is no doubt about it: God's providence takes care of those who trust in Him.

We can, however, take this further. The central mystery of the Christian faith, the passion, death and resurrection of the Lord, does it not show us that the greatest crime in history—the murder of the Son of God—can be turned by the Providence of God into the greatest good (the redemption of the human race)? To quote the immortal St Gregory once again:

> "The persecutors carried out what they strove to accomplish with pernicious intent and did him to death so that they might deprive him of the devotion of the faithful. Yet just where the cruel infidels thought they could extinguish faith, there faith grew. And when they thought they were rid of his miracles through persecution, they naturally compelled themselves unintentionally to increase them... Accordingly, in a wonderful way even that which happens without God's will is not contrary to God's will, because evil deeds are turned to a good purpose, and even when they are oriented against his plan, they are nevertheless made to act in accordance with it".[15]

---

[14] Mt 6:25-33.
[15] St Gregory the Great, ibid., p. 59.

If we seek to uncover the very root of this doctrine, we find ourselves going back to the revealed doctrine of creation *ex nihilo*. God alone can create, for to create something out of nothing is the prerogative of the sole divine power.[16] But what about *after* creation? Does God create and then leave the universe to itself? Or does He entrust it to others? St Thomas states unequivocally that God is the primary cause of every being, not only in the general concept of being, but also in its specificity, and even in its individuality. God alone can give being, and He alone presides over all that exists even down to the most minute detail. As the sun is the cause of light, so God is the essential and direct cause of all being. In other words, God is present and acting in all things: "God knows all things, both universal and particular. And since His knowledge may be compared to the thing as the knowledge of art to the objects of art..., all things must of necessity come under His ordering, just as all things wrought by art are subject to the ordering of that art".[17]

The universe, then, is a great work of art. Like every artist, God had something in mind when He created the world, for we know by experience that things act for the sake of an end. Natural things do this naturally, while free things do it intentionally. For example, the beaver makes a dam because it is naturally ordered to the building of dams, even though it has no knowledge of what it is doing. But beings endowed with intelligence act intentionally for an end. Men also build dams, but when they do so it is for a specific purpose, namely, saving water, or providing electrical power, etc. These a beaver will never do.

If the end of all things—an end which transcends all others—is the Divine Goodness, and if it belongs to Divine

---

[16] Cf. St Thomas Aquinas, *Summa Theologiae*, Ia, q. 45, a. 5.
[17] St Thomas Aquinas, *Summa Theologiae*, Ia, q. 22, a. 2, corpus. Here and elsewhere, all quotations from the *Summa Theologiae* are taken from the translation of the English Dominican Province.

Providence to produce the different types of beings, it follows that the first good of things, and one which is in the very heart of things themselves, is the perfection of the universe. The universe includes both visible and invisible beings. Since God, sovereign and immutable Being, is pure spirit, the more one approaches God, the more one approaches perfection. And so, pure spirits like angels are at the summit of the hierarchy of beings. Then comes man, the animals, the plants and finally the minerals. All these levels contribute to the harmony of the universe and proclaim the praise of the Creator.

Now, this perfection would not exist without various levels of being: "For to providence it belongs to order things towards an end. Now after the Divine Goodness, which is an end separate from all things, the principal good in things themselves is the perfection of the universe, which would not be, were not all grades of being found in things. Hence it pertains to Divine Providence to produce every grade of being".[18]

In reality, it is the whole of creation which realises the highest perfection, whereas each being in particular has a lesser perfection. This is the reason for which, when at the end of each day of creation (from the third to the sixth), "God saw that it was good",[19] whereas at the end of the sixth day, He saw that it was "very good". St John Chrysostom bases himself on this word of Genesis to put an end to all curious investigation into God's purposes:

> "After the things which were created had come to be and each thing had received its proper form, Moses shows the Creator praising every created thing, or rather, each thing singly and everything together, so that,

---

[18] St Thomas Aquinas, *Summa Theologiae*, Ia, q. 22, a. 4, corpus.
[19] Gen 1:10, 12, 18, 21, 25, 31.

knowing the Creator's estimation, no one—even if he were exceedingly reckless and shameless—would pry further into visible things. Therefore, having said that the light came to be, he adds: 'And God saw the light, that it was good', and likewise for each thing. Then, so as not to draw out his discourse by mentioning everything by name, he gives an account of everything in general at the same time and says: 'God saw everything that He had made, and behold, it was very good'... Therefore, since you have such testimony of their excellence, do not be inquisitive, and do not pry curiously into created things".[20]

If God created all things to be good, we can say that, since love tends towards what is good, God "loved things into existence". If he had not loved, they would not be. Love is found at the very heart of all being.

We are now faced with another question: If God looks after everything, if His wisdom disposes of all with love, does this mean that things happen of necessity, and that there is no real freedom among created beings? Would the entire universe and its history then be nothing more than an immense, and often tragic, puppet show? What happens to the freedom of creatures?

Here St Thomas Aquinas gives us an answer that is far-reaching in its implications and unsurpassed in the annals of human thought. It is true, he writes, that God, and God alone, produces all things. He does this however, in various ways, for some of His creatures act of necessity, others by contingency, each in its own way. The sun rises of necessity in the

---

[20] St John Chrysostom, *On the Providence of God*, ch. 4, translation by Monk Moses, St Herman of Alaska Brotherhood, 2015, pp. 47-49.

sense that it is made—today we would say "programmed"—to do so and does not have a choice. Peter, on the other hand, waters his garden by contingency, for he has free will and could simply refuse to do it. There is nothing in Peter or in nature that would make his watering the garden inevitable. If he does not, it is not the end of the world. This diversity, while it shows the richness of the universal cause which is God, is in no way opposed to the fact that God governs all: "The order of Divine Providence is unchangeable and certain, so far as all things which are provided for by Him happen as they have been provided for, whether from necessity or from contingency".[21] God alone is able to give to rational creatures to be free, to respect their choices, and at the same time to be at work in the very actions and choices they make, even those which are contrary to Him, at least insofar as He gives them the very being which they use against Him.

This brings us to our next chapter on the role of creatures in the realisation of God's plan.

---

[21] St Thomas Aquinas, *Summa Theologiae*, Ia, q. 22, a. 4, ad 2.

2
Providence and its Co-Workers

"That we may be fellow helpers of the truth".[1]

GOD IS THE cause of all that exists: this is the dogma of creation. He is also the cause of all that is accomplished in the universe: this is the dogma of conservation, of which providence is a part. In causing things to happen, however, God ordinarily acts through creatures who also become causes. A few examples: the acorn produces an oak, the horse begets a horse, man and woman procreate another human, etc.

Because God is the universal cause, and because He has given creatures to be causes also, theology has developed the terminology of referring to God as the "primary cause" and to creatures as "secondary causes", in the sense that they are both efficient causes of things. We call creatures secondary causes because, in the very act of causing an effect, the creature is moved by another cause, the primary cause, which is God. Let's take an example. When a stick, held by a man, strikes a rock and moves it, the stick is secondary cause of the movement of the rock, the man being the primary cause. The action and the causality of the secondary cause depend upon the primary cause: if there were no man, there would be no movement of

---

[1] 3 Jn 1:8.

the stick towards the rock. The stick could do nothing on its own, for the movement flows from the primary cause through the secondary cause to move the rock.

Let's stop here for a moment and consider some of the consequences of this doctrine. By allowing creatures to cause things in their turn, to be real and true causes, God gives them an astounding dignity. He is actually inviting them to be His co-workers and He is thus sharing with them some of His power. His providence looks over all things without intermediary, that is to say, directly, for everything that exists and is done is seen by Him; whenever He assigns certain effects to certain causes, these causes become His intermediaries. This is not due to any defect in His power, but "by reason of the abundance of His goodness, so that the dignity of causality is imparted even to creatures".[2]

This point cannot be overly stressed. If God alone can create, that is to say, produce being out of nothing, it is because He alone is primary cause of all things. There are secondary causes, that is to say, beings which are true causes of others and of things, but in total dependence on the primary cause. The secondary causes, however perfect they may be, can in no way call other beings into existence. They cannot create. They can only cooperate to produce another being according to the measure they themselves have received. For example, birds make nests in which they lay their eggs and feed their young. They do not research better methods for building better nests! A bird will never build a dam or write a book. The only attitude which is becoming of the secondary cause is therefore that of receptivity, openness to the primary cause under whose influence it achieves what it has been given to achieve at every moment. But the causality of a secondary cause is a real and

---

[2] St Thomas Aquinas, *Summa Theologiae,* Ia, q. 22, a. 3, corpus.

true cause with a real influence of its own on the end effect. When a person writes a poem with a blue pen, the poem that is written is in blue ink. It's a blue poem.

St Thomas will go so far as to say, referring to those beings that are able to transmit being to others (as when a horse begets a horse or a man begets a man) that "all things that give being do so because they act by God's power".[3] In other words, it is the very power of God of which the creature is making use in its action, inasmuch as, in every one of them, it actually draws from the primary source. It is, we could say, as if there were an infinite ocean of energy which is God, and from which every creature draws whenever it does anything at all. St Ignatius of Loyola was hinting at this when, at the end of the Spiritual Exercises, he invites the retreatant to consider that God is labouring in all things for him: "Consider how God works and labours for me in all creatures upon the face of the earth, that is, He conducts Himself as one who labours. Thus, in the heavens, the elements, the plants, the fruits, the cattle, etc., He gives being, conserves them, confers life and sensation, etc".[4] Labouring He is indeed, in and through the very labour of man!

However, among creatures, some are gifted with reason, and in this capacity they share more closely in the causality which takes its entire source from God. Let's look at an example. There is a big difference between animal copulation and human procreation. The former is ordered towards the propagation of the species by the natural instinct of which the animal is not aware. Horses do not understand why they copulate, nor do they know that eleven months later a foal will be born, nor do they discuss the size of the family they want to

---

[3] St Thomas Aquinas, *Summa contra Gentiles* B. 3, ch. 66. Here and elsewhere quotations from the third book of *Summa contra Gentiles* are taken from the translation by Vernon J. Bourke.
[4] St Ignatius of Loyola, *Spiritual Exercises* no. 236.

found! Human procreation is at an entirely different level—or should be at least—in that humans know to what their actions lead and at least some of the consequences they will have. This, by the way, is one of the reasons for which contraception is wrong: it is impossible for a rational being to perform an action without wanting the end of that action, unless he/she is lying. Now, the sexual act, of its very nature, is ordered towards the transmission of life, so to engage in it while refusing its life-giving capacity is essentially a lie. The inbuilt language of sex is the total gift of self, including the spouses capacity to give and receive life. But contraception layers over the top of this another language: I refuse to give/receive life in my action and therefore I do not totally give myself to the other person. So in the body we say one thing (nature's language) but in the intention we say another (conception).[5]

St Thomas summarises the different ways of taking part in providence between rational and irrational creatures by saying that "some beings so exist as God's products that, possessing understanding, they bear His likeness and reflect His image. Consequently, they are not only ruled but are also rulers of

---

[5] Pope St John Paul II made this point in his Apostolic Exhortation *Familiaris consortio*, 32: "When couples, by means of recourse to contraception, separate these two meanings that God the Creator has inscribed in the being of man and woman and in the dynamism of their sexual communion, they act as 'arbiters' of the divine plan and they 'manipulate' and degrade human sexuality—and with it themselves and their married partner—by altering its value of 'total' self-giving. Thus the innate language that expresses the total reciprocal self-giving of husband and wife is overlaid, through contraception, by an objectively contradictory language, namely, that of not giving oneself totally to the other. This leads not only to a positive refusal to be open to life but also to a falsification of the inner truth of conjugal love, which is called upon to give itself in personal totality."

themselves, inasmuch as their own actions are directed to a fitting end".[6] Now, if God truly gives creatures to be causes, does this diminish His role? Far from it. The causality of creatures actually puts divine causality into sharper perspective. How so? A government whose goal is to lead governed beings to perfection, will be all the better when a greater perfection is communicated to these beings by the one who governs.

If God concerns Himself directly and immediately with everything that happens in the universe, He does so through intermediaries. This is the meaning of the dictum *de minimis non curat praetor—Trivial matters are no concern of a high official.* The higher one is lifted up, the more one uses the service of ministers to execute details. The renowned French Marshal Ferdinand Foch put it this way: *Ne rien faire; tout faire faire; ne rien laisser faire—do nothing; get others to do everything; let no one get away with anything.*

But if it is true that rulers use intermediaries, their lack of direct knowledge of all things is a sign of their limits and weakness. In other words, if the human leader uses intermediaries, it is simply because it is humanly impossible for him to look after everything. This however, can in no way be said of God: "It pertains to a king's dignity to have ministers who execute his providence. But the fact that he has not the plan of those things which are done by them arises from a deficiency in himself. For every operative science is the more perfect the more it considers the particular things with which its action is concerned".[7] This way of acting is demanded by the divine perfection, which created all degrees of being. Now, at the summit, there are those who participate in what is absolutely

---

[6] St Thomas Aquinas, *Summa contra Gentiles*, B. 3, ch. 1.
[7] St Thomas Aquinas, *Summa Theologiae*, Ia, q. 22, a. 3, ad 1.

speaking the most perfect, that is to say, the capacity to understand and to will, and thus to order other beings to their end.

Why did God make things this way? Because, if creatures did not have to a certain extent this capacity to be efficient, then the excellence of the world would be greatly diminished. In the same way that it is proper to the sovereign being to communicate His goodness by doing good, in the same way His goodness reaches a summit by giving to creatures the capacity to do good in their turn.

> "The ability to make an actual thing results from being actually existent, as is evident in the case of God, for He is pure act and is also the first cause of being for all things… Therefore, if He has communicated His likeness, as far as actual being is concerned, to other things, by virtue of the fact that He has brought things into being, it follows that He has communicated to them His likeness, as far as acting is concerned, so that created things may also have their own actions. Furthermore, the perfection of the effect demonstrates the perfection of the cause, for a greater power brings about a more perfect effect. But God is the most perfect agent. Therefore, things created by Him obtain perfection from Him. So, to detract from the perfection of creatures is to detract from the perfection of divine power".[8]

Let's read that again: To detract from the perfection of creatures is to detract from the perfection of divine power. This is precisely why Satan is so relentless in his ferocious attacks on the human race. He hates God, but can do nothing to hurt Him, so he turns on His creatures, knowing full well the

---

[8] St Thomas Aquinas, *Summa contra Gentiles*, B. 3, ch. 69.

dignity God has put in them and seeking thereby to cancel out God's work by cancelling out His creatures, and in this way, as it were, to try to cancel out God.

Up to now we have seen that God is the first and universal cause who provides directly for all that happens in creation; secondary causes have real influence and are strictly speaking causes. Now we must explain the relation between primary cause and secondary cause. In other words, must one attribute to God everything, including the free actions of secondary causes, in which case, do we not run the risk of reducing the latter to the role of puppets? Or rather must we acknowledge that rational creatures really do have free and personal initiative, in which case do we not deprive God of the prerogative of being the universal cause of all things?

St Thomas Aquinas frequently reverts in his writing to the solution he gives to this problem, namely that everything one can attribute to the secondary cause, must be attributed even more to the primary cause. "God operates continually in the mind," he writes, "since He causes and governs the natural light in it, and thus the mind does not carry on its own function without the operation of the First Cause".[9] In the very act of thinking, a rational creature benefits from the direct influence of God, without whose light he could understand nothing, according to the prologue of St John's Gospel: The Word "was the true light, which enlighteneth every man that cometh into this world".[10]

Does God use rational creatures as a man uses a stick purely and simply, in which case He would be imposing causality? No. One must distinguish between secondary instrumental cause (the stick used by the man) and the secondary principal cause (the worker who builds a house under the orders of the

---

[9] St Thomas Aquinas, *Super Boetium in Trinitate*, q. 1, a. 1, ad 6. Translation by Rose E. Brennan.

[10] Jn 1:9.

architect). While the instrumental cause acts only by virtue of the principal agent, the secondary principle cause acts by its own power.[11] Note what was said earlier about the pen having its own proper effect, even though it is by virtue of the person writing with it, otherwise the blue ink marks on the paper would be incoherent. But since the person writes a poem with the pen, the effect is blue ink marks that are words with syntax and meaning. Thus the primary efficient cause, the poet, elevates and applies the pen to do something that of itself it is incapable of (even though it has what we call an "obediential potency"—that is to say that it has the power to lend itself to a higher agent which it "obeys". In this case, the pen "obeys" the poet and thus becomes a dependent cause of what may become a masterpiece.

In other words, the primary cause influences rational creatures in a way that is in conformity with their nature. Since this nature is gifted with an intellect and free will, the influx of the primary cause respects this reality. "It would be incompatible with providence for that whereby a thing attains the divine likeness to be taken away from it. Now, the voluntary agent attains the divine likeness because it acts freely, for… there is free choice in God. Therefore, freedom of will is not taken away by Divine Providence".[12]

This principle establishes with clarity the extension and limits of secondary causes. The more the primary cause influences others, the loftier will they be, the more will they know of the divine plan and the more will they use intermediaries to effect their full potential as causes. The same principle allows one to establish the nobility and dignity of each secondary cause, since the number and diversity of ministers is the sign of a greater dignity in the leader.

---

[11] Cf. for example St Thomas Aquinas, *De Veritate*, q. 27, a. 4.
[12] St Thomas Aquinas, *Summa contra Gentiles*, B. 3, ch. 73.

A distinction must here be made between the influence a secondary cause has on irrational creatures and that which it exerts over rational creatures. Given that harmonious order is a descent by degrees from superior to inferior beings, it is manifest that the latter will be governed by the former. Rational creatures partake in effect of the double cognitive and efficient power of God. St Thomas will even say that each spiritual nature is in some way all things according to the measure in which its intelligence embraces all things; in the same way, the spiritual nature being destined to remain always, it is willed for itself, whereas irrational creatures are willed for it; it is therefore normal that it preside over the destiny of other creatures. For example, one art, which is concerned with the end from which the plan for the entire artistic production is derived, directs and commands other arts which make the product. It is the art of navigation which inspires the art of shipbuilding. Since only intellectual creatures can know the rational plans for the ordering of creatures, it will be their function to rule and govern all other creatures. They motivate and regulate them.[13] One author puts it this way:

> "In a real way, one must admit that spiritual causes, being superior to the material ones as to their being, ... surpass them equally in the domain of action. This superiority in perfection of spiritual creatures over bodies in the dynamic order flows from the freedom of the will, by which these creatures must choose their last end and realise the effective pursuit of it with corresponding means".[14]

---

[13] Cf. St Thomas Aquinas, *Summa contra Gentiles* B. 3, ch. 78.
[14] C. Fabro, C.P.S., *Participation et causalité selon saint Thomas d'Aquin*, Publications universitaires de Louvain, 1961. p. 49. Translation mine.

However, the task remains of reconciling the divine action, which is preponderant, with human or angelic action, which is subordinate. Aquinas is here able to bring his teaching to yet another and even loftier summit which remains one of those unequalled monuments of human thought. As is his custom, he begins by summarising the *objection,* to which he will respond later: since the divine power suffices to produce natural effects, it is useless to appeal to the capacities of nature; if nature suffices to produce an effect, there is no need for the divine power; besides, "nature does not use two instruments when one suffices". In other words, either God or the creature is cause, but they cannot both be at the same time.

Aquinas *replies* that such a reasoning does not hold. In fact, if we take the example of a worker who uses an instrument to perform some task, it is clear that he gives this instrument to be the secondary immediate cause, as he himself is the primary immediate cause of what it produces. So, both the worker and the tool are both integral cause of the whole work. St Thomas continues:

> "It is also evident that, though a natural thing produces its proper effect, it is not superfluous for God to produce it, since the natural thing does not produce it except by divine power. Nor is it superfluous, even if God can by Himself produce all natural effects, for them to be produced by certain other causes. For this is not a result of the inadequacy of divine power, but of the immensity of His goodness, whereby He has willed to communicate His likeness to things, not only so that they might exist, but also that they might be causes for other things. Indeed, all creatures generally attain the divine likeness in these two ways... By this, in fact, the beauty of order in created things is evident. It is

also apparent that the same effect is not attributed to a natural cause and to divine power in such a way that it is partly done by God, and partly by the natural agent; rather, it is wholly done by both, according to a different way, just as the same effect is wholly attributed to the instrument and also wholly to the principal agent".[15]

This reply of the Angelic Doctor, in which we find the famous formula: *totus ab utroque*—wholly done by both—, leaves God and man their respective essential roles in every human act and in the unfolding of human history. And here we can take the full measure of the dignity of the secondary cause, granted by God to the rational creature. Man holds his own destiny and that of others in his hand: he must prove himself worthy of his calling.

The same doctrine is to be found in the teaching of St Thomas on the human will. An objector advances two texts of Scripture: "As the divisions of waters, so the heart of the king is in the hand of the Lord: whithersoever he will, he shall turn it",[16] and "For it is God who worketh in you, both to will and to accomplish, according to his good will".[17] If it is so, the *objector* holds, man is not free; he is therefore not a cause in the strict sense of the term. In his *response*, Aquinas affirms that nothing prevents the will from being free, even though it is not its own primary cause. There can only be one primary cause, God, and He it is who impresses all movement upon beings: "Just as by moving natural causes He does not prevent their acts being natural, so by moving voluntary causes He does not deprive their actions of being voluntary, but rather is He the cause of this very thing in them; for He operates in each thing according

---

[15] St Thomas Aquinas, *Summa contra Gentiles*, B. 3, ch. 70.
[16] Proverbs 21:1.
[17] Phil 2:13.

to its own nature".[18] And with his usual concision in the commentary on the Gospel of St John: "God works in us, but not without us... What is produced in me by God is also produced in me by myself, that is, by my free choice".[19] In other words, God freely moves us to move freely. There is no competition between God as first cause and all creaturely causes.

In this luminous solution to one of the hardest problems, we can already see the place of prayer and study to which St Thomas attaches such importance. By means of prayer, as we shall see in chapter four, a person works together with God to make things happen which might otherwise never be. By means of study, a person furthers the grasp he or she has of the universe and thus takes part in bringing it to perfection. We also see the importance of virtue, for by not being virtuous one falls into sin which is opposed to the very plan God's providence has over the universe. The sinner, in some way, seeks to act independently of the primary cause, and to establish himself as an autonomous cause, but this is impossible, for every creature is utterly dependent upon the Creator.

The analogy with the master who orders must be completed by that of the master who teaches. If speculative knowledge is all the more perfect when it has to do with universals (for this is more knowable in itself), it is no less true that the one who has a more specific knowledge of things possesses a more perfect knowledge of them. So it is that the student, from general knowledge, arrives at a more specific knowledge, thanks to the help of his teacher. A fortiori, on the level of practical knowledge, the one who has detailed knowledge of beings has consummate knowledge of things. So it is for God. But this also flows from the fact that the entire universe is ordered

---

[18] St Thomas Aquinas, *Summa Theologiae*, Ia, q. 83, a. 1, ad 3.
[19] St Thomas Aquinas, *Lecture on the Gospel of John*, c. 14, l. 3. Translation by Fabian R. Larcher, O.P.

to the Divine Bounty: "since all things are ordered to divine goodness as an end, it follows that God, to Whom this goodness primarily belongs, as something substantially possessed and known and loved, must be the governor of all things".[20]

We might ask: Why is this the case? St Thomas comes to our help again by making yet another very enlightening distinction between the two constitutive elements of providence, namely God's plan and its execution. The plan, or thought in the Divine Mind, is all the more perfect in that it embraces even the most minute details. It is indeed a sign of the greatest intelligence when someone can embrace the entirety of a large project. Is this not what astounds us the most in the forming of a vast architectural complex, the plot of an exciting novel, or the fine nuances of a classical symphony? The execution of the plan, however, will be more perfect when it is exercised through intermediaries, and the more numerous the intermediaries, the greater the talent in harmonising their roles. In fact, the more intelligent the leader, the more will he be concerned with the details of those who are in submission to him, but the less he will intervene directly; for the higher he is, the less becoming it is that he bend over to insignificant details. "He Himself through His wisdom must arrange the orders for all things, even the least; on the other hand, He may execute the small details by means of other lower powers, through which He Himself works, as does a universal and higher power through a lower and particular power. It is appropriate, then, that there be inferior agents as executors of Divine Providence".[21]

Not as easy to understand, especially for our contemporary mentality imbued with individual autonomy, is the extension of this principle to rational creatures themselves. St Thomas

---

[20] St Thomas Aquinas, *Summa contra Gentiles*, B. 3, ch. 64.
[21] St Thomas Aquinas, *Summa contra Gentiles*, B. 3, ch. 77.

is however clear on this point: the entire universe is ordered; the creatures closest to the primary cause exert a secondary causality over those that are further from it. Now, there are essentially two types of intellectual creatures, angels and men. Angels are superior to men, and that is why they preside over the destiny of the latter:

> "Superior intellectual substances receive the influence of divine wisdom into themselves more perfectly, because each being receives something according to the being's own mode. Now, all things are governed by divine wisdom. And so, things that participate more in divine wisdom must be capable of governing those that participate less. Therefore, the lower intellectual substances are governed by the higher ones. Thus, the higher spirits are also called angels, because they direct the lower spirits, as it were, by bringing messages to them; in fact, angels are spoken of as messengers. And they are also called ministers, because they carry out by their operation the order of Divine Providence even in the area of bodily things. Indeed, a minister is like a living instrument".[22]

The fact that God deputes His angels to lead men to their eternal destiny is in no way a sign of weakness, as if He could not do so Himself. In reality, it is due to the order of His wisdom. There are two reasons for this: the first is that it is becoming that this dignity of being divine co-workers be attributed to the angels inasmuch as they are the leaders and the guides of men; the second is that men are in a state of imperfection with regard to angels; they are like children who see only in

---

[22] St Thomas Aquinas, *Summa contra Gentiles*, B. 3, ch. 79.

part, but in Heaven they will see as they are seen.[23] Here we can also see the application of another principle: providence lets each thing act according to its nature, for it seeks to preserve the capacities of each nature, not to destroy them.[24]

But the principle actually goes further. Men too are rational creatures and therefore they are providence for themselves: "God leaves man in the hand of his own counsel, because He gives him providence over his own acts".[25] St Thomas is only paraphrasing Holy Scripture here: "God made man from the beginning, and left him in the hand of his own counsel".[26] This principle works in both directions: each man is called to be providence for himself, that is to say, "prevenient", or rather, prudent, in the way he leads his life. But among men, some are proposed for teaching and governing others. Here too, as for the angels, it is not at all because of the weakness or personal incapacity that God has recourse to this means, but to ennoble them.

We might at this stage ask why it is that God acts this way. Why does He not direct everything directly? Two main reasons come immediately to mind. The first is what we call the principle of the *generosity of the act*; if God chooses freely the mediation of secondary causes, it is thus that He manifests His supreme liberality by giving men to participate in His goodness:

> "God wanted to have certain witnesses, not because He needed their testimony, but to ennoble those whom He appointed witnesses. Thus we see in the order of the universe that God produces certain effects by means of

---

[23] Cf. St Thomas Aquinas, *II Sent.* d. 11, q. 1, a. 1, ad 1, with reference to 1 Co 13:9-12.
[24] Ibid, d. 23, q. 1, a. 2, corpus: *Non corruptiva naturae, sed salvativa*.
[25] St Thomas Aquinas, *De Veritate*, q. 5, a. 5, ad 4. Translation by Robert W. Mulligan, S.J.
[26] Sir 15:14.

intermediate causes, not because He Himself is unable to produce them without these intermediaries, but He deigns to confer on them the dignity of causality because He wishes to ennoble these intermediate causes. Similarly, even though God could have enlightened all men by Himself and lead them to a knowledge of Himself, yet to preserve due order in things and to ennoble certain men, He willed that divine knowledge reach men through certain other men".[27]

The second reason is the *proportion between cause and effect*. The good teacher wants to lead his students to his own level, but often he cannot do so alone. He sometimes uses an intermediary, such as a tutor, who is closer to the student and can more easily convey the message. "Certain men of weak understanding are unable to grasp the truth and knowledge of God by themselves. And so the Lord chose to come down to them and to enlighten certain men before others about divine matters, so that these others might obtain from them in a human way the knowledge of divine things they could not reach by themselves".[28]

God Himself acted this way when He sent His Son to take flesh and so be our Master and Guide. Christ in turn chose men, first the apostles to whom he revealed His plans and whom He established as doctors of the faith. Enlightened by Christ, these become light for other men. St Thomas makes it clear that the apostle is an "enlightened light"—*lux illuminata*; indeed, only Christ is the "true light who enlightens every man—*lux vera qui illuminat omnem hominem*" (Jn 1:9). But having been enlightened by Christ, the apostle is henceforth capable in turn of enlightening others.

---

[27] St Thomas Aquinas, *Lecture on the Gospel of John*, c. 1, l. 4. Translation by James A. Weisheipl, O.P.
[28] St Thomas Aquinas, ibid.

Another concept dear to Aquinas is that it is better to enlighten than merely to shine—*maius est illuminare quam lucere solum*.[29] In the same way, in another passage, where this question is carved in stone, summarised in a formula that one can consider to be a self-portrait of the holy doctor, we can perceive all the vigour of the dynamic spirituality which flows from it: "It is a greater perfection for a thing to be good in itself and also the cause of goodness in others, than only to be good in itself. Therefore God so governs things that He makes some of them to be causes of others in government; as a master, who not only imparts knowledge to his pupils, but also makes them teachers of others".[30]

Among men, there is a very special category which is the saints already in the heavenly homeland. They are assimilated to the angels in this that God uses them as intermediaries to lead their brothers and sisters to beatitude. They have become in an eminent way providence for themselves and for others.[31]

But this family of God in the eternal homeland is already commenced in this world through the Church. Christ did not choose to remain visibly present in the world, which He could very well have done. He chose instead to ascend into Heaven, and from there to make Himself present to all generations and peoples through the Church, its hierarchy and its sacraments. What was visible in Christ has passed into the sacraments, said Pope St Leo the Great.[32] We could also say that what was providence in Christ has passed to the Church, the family of God on earth.

Finally, the family of God is also mirrored in some way by the domestic church which is the family. When a child comes

---

[29] St Thomas Aquinas, *Summa Theologiae*, IIa-IIae, q. 188, a. 6, corpus.
[30] St Thomas Aquinas, *Summa Theologiae*, Ia, q. 103, a. 6, corpus.
[31] Cf. St Thomas Aquinas, *IV Sent*. d. 49, q. 1, a. 2, qc. 5, ad 3.
[32] St Leo the Great, *Sermon 74 for the Ascension*.

into the world, he does so as the most helpless of creatures, utterly dependent upon his progenitors. The providence of God is relayed to the little human by means of those who brought him into the world, along with the help of many others (doctors, nurses, teachers, tutors, coaches, etc.). Only after many years of learning through others can he then become providence in his turn.

A recent author summarised this doctrine in this way:

> "The fact that God acts through creatures does not diminish in any way their proper role. On the contrary. Not only does God will and act, but He also makes to will and to act. He has beings take part not only in what He is but also in what He does. Not only in His being and action, but also in His thought and in His love: in His providence. Undoubtedly it is partial, and many are the secondary causes which God puts into motion for a single effect willed by Him. And especially, says St Thomas, the primary Cause moves much further in producing the effect than do the secondary causes. It alone remains. When the secondary cause is a man, when it is a matter of producing by means of it a supernatural effect, a work of salvation, then the word of the Lord is realised. 'I will not now call you servants: for the servant knoweth not what his lord doth. But I have called you friends, because all things, whatsoever I have heard of my Father, I have made known to you… I have chosen you; and have appointed you, that you should go and should bring forth fruit…' (Jn 15: 15-16)".[33]

---

[33] M.-J. Nicolas, O.P. *Croire en la providence?* Pierre Téqui (1995) 91-92. Translation mine.

Is this not what Our Lord meant to convey when He told us the parable of the vine? "Abide in me: and I in you. As the branch cannot bear fruit of itself, unless it abide in the vine, so neither can you, unless you abide in me. I am the vine: you the branches. He that abideth in me, and I in him, the same beareth much fruit: for without me you can do nothing".[34] Without the Lord we can do nothing, for without Him we would not even exist, and here we see that this doctrine also grounds us in the virtue of humility. But with Him we "can do all things",[35] for we have been given the amazing capacity of working together with Divine Providence who has loved us so much.

Here we can get a glimpse of the staggering depth of God's love for us. In choosing us for collaborators and making us His friends, He wants to share with us the amazing capacity to lead other creatures to their ultimate destiny. But we know also that there are many hurdles along the way. There is evil in the world and what appear to be chance events which disrupt our lives. How do these fit in with the dogma of Divine Providence?

---

[34] Jn 15:4-5.
[35] Ph 4:13.

3
Providence, Evil and Chance

If evil exists, God exists.[1]

THE AFFIRMATION OF the existence of God and His providence immediately gives rise to a question which no generation has been able to avoid: if God the Creator is so good and so provident, how is it that there is evil in the universe? St Thomas, always a fair debater, evokes the following *objection*: "A wise provider excludes any defect or evil, as far as he can, from those over whom he has a care. But we see many evils existing. Either, then, God cannot hinder these, and thus is not omnipotent; or else He does not have care for everything".[2] Bad things happen. So either there is no God, or God is not omnipotent, or He doesn't really care. So goes the *objection*.

When a being is in charge of a particular good, points out St Thomas, he does all that he can to exclude from it every defect and avoid any destruction of what is entrusted to his keep. But the one who has a higher charge, sees the good of the whole of things and can allow what appears evil for one, in the measure that it serves the good of another and consequently of all. An example will help us illustrate this point. A cattle-breeder takes great care of his cattle, making sure they have the right feed and water, and that they are protected from illness and death,

---

[1] St Thomas Aquinas, *Summa contra Gentiles*, B. 3, ch. 71.
[2] St Thomas Aquinas, *Summa Theologiae*, Ia, q. 22, a. 2, obj 2.

for his work is to bring the animals to their perfection for the common good. The butcher, however, is not concerned with the animals' lives; he actually wants dead cattle, for what he is interested in is the beef that will allow him to feed people. The physical evil of killing the cattle is for the profit of human beings. And the whole operation,—farmer, butcher, consumer—is overseen by the one who has the responsibility of the common good of the state. The example given by St Thomas is closer to nature: the fox eats the rabbit, and this keeps the rabbits from becoming too numerous and devouring men's crops. In the universe, all things are within an order. The disappearance of one favours the growth of another.

The perfection of the universe demands a diversity of beings. Now this diversity includes, of necessity, a certain hierarchy of goods, and whoever says hierarchy of goods, says that certain ones are better than others and, consequently, certain ones appear evil with regard to others. If this "evil" is suppressed, it would mean the suppression of the hierarchy and therefore the diversity: there would no longer be any harmony of the whole.

This being said, we must accept not being always able to understand the place of certain apparent physical evils in the world. In the face of those who criticise God for what they perceive as problems in the universe, St John Chrysostom has this to say:

> "I mean that it is ridiculous to think that someone without knowledge and without experience would ask the Artisan the reasons for everything that He brings about, that he would be inquisitive about this unspeakable, unutterable, inexpressible, and incomprehensible Wisdom, and that he would inquire into why such and such has come to be, knowing clearly that this Wisdom is infallible, that His goodness is great, that His providence is indescribable, and that everything that comes to us

from Him is completely to our benefit—provided our own actions do not interfere—since He does not want anyone to perish, but rather wants to save them. How is it not exceeding folly to inquisitively question at the outset and right away Him who wishes and is able to save everyone—and not wait for the final outcome of events?"[3]

What about natural disasters? Are these caused by God? To answer that question, let's ask another one: If God did not cause it, who did? If God is who we say He is, it is certain that He is almighty and omniscient. If He is almighty, He could have prevented it from happening. If He is omniscient, He knows exactly when and where it will happen. In either case, His allowing awful things to happen would mean either that He is not omnipotent or not omniscient, or that He is downright evil. Unless we can admit that maybe, just maybe, there is a reason for it that we are not aware of. Ultimately therefore, one must accept either that God is not omnipotent—which is heresy, being opposed to the very first article of the Creed (*I believe in God the Father Almighty*) or that God could have done something about it and did not and therefore that He is at the very least the indirect cause of it. This can only mean that yes, God is responsible for natural disasters.

Why does He allow them or even directly cause them? That is not always comprehensible for us, even though Holy Scripture makes it clear that sometimes they are chastisements positively willed by God. God wants people to convert and sometimes the only way to achieve such a conversion is to wake them up from their spiritual torpor by means of an earthquake, a fire, a tsunami, a pandemic, etc.

---

[3] St John Chrysostom, *On the Providence of God*, ch. 8, translation by Monk Moses, St Herman of Alaska Brotherhood, 2015, pp. 75-76.

One example among legion is God's words to Moses:

> "If you ... contemn my judgments so as not to do those things which are appointed by me, and to make void my covenant... I will quickly visit you with poverty, and burning heat, which shall waste your eyes, and consume your lives. You shall sow your seed in vain, which shall be devoured by your enemies. I will set my face against you, and you shall fall down before your enemies: and shall be made subject to them that hate you... I will break the pride of your stubbornness ... If you walk contrary to me, and will not hearken to me, ... I will send in upon you the beasts of the field, to destroy you and your cattle, and make you few in number... I will bring in upon you the sword that shall avenge my covenant. And when you shall flee into the cities, I will send the pestilence in the midst of you. And you shall be delivered into the hands of your enemies".[4]

There is the specific case in the life of King David in which God sends a pestilence to punish Israel and its king.[5] Of course, as Our Lord Himself warned us, we must not draw too quickly the conclusion that because an earthquake or a tsunami or pestilence or extreme poverty plague a particular area, the people who live there are more sinful than others:

> "And there were present, at that very time, some that told him of the Galileans, whose blood Pilate had mingled with their sacrifices. And he answering, said to them: Think you that these Galileans were sinners above all the men of Galilee, because they suffered such things?

---

[4] Lev 26:14-25.
[5] Cf. 2 Sam 24 and 1 Chron 21.

No, I say to you: but unless you shall do penance, you shall all likewise perish. Or those eighteen upon whom the tower fell in Siloe and slew them: think you that they also were debtors above all the men that dwelt in Jerusalem? No, I say to you: but except you do penance, you shall all likewise perish".[6]

But the fact remains: such disasters can very well be a punishment for sin, the primary goal of which is to correct the sinner. In any case, punishment or not, such events are certainly destined to lift up the minds and hearts of those who experience them and those who are aware of them to the higher realm of the spirit and eternal life. The greatest lesson these happenings teach us is that we are not here to stay. Nothing is more appropriate for bringing this truth home to us than events which cause the limited order of our little world to fall apart. God does sometimes positively will physical evils so that a moral good may come from them.

But does really God punish? Does He chastise? The answer to that question is given to us by God Himself: "For whom the Lord loveth he chastiseth: and he scourgeth every son whom he receiveth. Persevere under discipline. God dealeth with you as with his sons. For what son is there whom the father doth not correct? But if you be without chastisement, whereof all are made partakers, then are you bastards and not sons".[7] It simply will not do to say, every time something bad happens, that it is not a punishment from God. Who are we to say such a thing? Especially when we have numerous incidents in Sacred Scripture that depict an infinitely good God as causing some

---

[6] Lk 13:1-5.
[7] Heb 12:6-8.

physical evil in order to punish and call to conversion. One of the most poignant is the prayer of Azarias:

> "Blessed art thou, O Lord, the God of our fathers,… for Thou art just in all that Thou hast done to us… For Thou hast executed true judgments in all the things that Thou hast brought upon us…, for according to truth and judgment, Thou hast brought all these things upon us for our sins. For we have sinned, and committed iniquity, departing from Thee: and we have trespassed in all things: and we have not hearkened to Thy commandments, nor have we observed nor done as Thou hadst commanded us, that it might go well with us. Wherefore, all that Thou hast brought upon us, and every thing that Thou hast done to us, Thou hast done in true judgment: and Thou hast delivered us into the hands of our enemies that are unjust, and most wicked…"[8]

All this goes, of course, for physical evil. But what shall we say of moral evil, of sin? Here, things are different, because God cannot be the primary cause of sin. Only creatures, that is, angels and human beings, can do that. So how are we to explain the presence of moral evil in a world under the governance of God? This question requires much more than a quick reply. The *Catechism of the Catholic Church* offers this consideration:

> "Only Christian faith as a whole constitutes the answer to this question: the goodness of creation, the drama of sin and the patient love of God who comes to meet man by his covenants, the redemptive Incarnation of his Son, his gift of the Spirit, his gathering of the

---

[8] Dan 3:26-33.

Church, the power of the sacraments and his call to a blessed life to which free creatures are invited to consent in advance, but from which, by a terrible mystery, they can also turn away in advance. There is not a single aspect of the Christian message that is not in part an answer to the question of evil".[9]

Indeed, the most definitive response was long ago formulated and summarised by St Augustine in this famous text: "For almighty God..., because He is supremely good, would never allow any evil whatsoever to exist in His works if He were not so all-powerful and good as to cause good to emerge from evil itself".[10] We already mentioned the case of the brothers of the Patriarch Joseph. They had evil intentions against him, but their evil was turned into good. Consider also the following examples.

The enslavement of the Hebrew people by the Egyptian Pharaoh and his refusal to let them go to offer sacrifice in the desert leads God to take them out definitively from Egypt and establish them in the promised land. To offset the moral evil of enslavement of the Hebrews, God inflicts physical evils (the ten plagues) on the Egyptians in order to further the loving plans of His providence.

The persecution of St Paul by the Jews forces him to appeal to Rome. This will take him to the Eternal City where he will preach the Gospel and shed his blood, thus adding his own witness to that of St Peter and establishing for all ages the pre-eminence of the Church of Rome. Indeed, in general, the evil of the persecution of the just by the wicked only serves to increase the patience and merits of the former.[11]

---

[9] *Catechism of the Catholic Church*, 309. A larger extract from the *Catechism* on Divine Providence and evil can be found in the appendix.
[10] St Augustine, *Enchiridion*, 11.
[11] Cf. St Thomas Aquinas, *Summa contra Gentiles*, B. 3, ch. 71.

Boethius adds an interesting comment to the effect that Divine Providence actually uses the extreme wickedness of some men to bring back to righteousness men who are less evil than they. These latter, by being treated unjustly at the hands of men much worse than they, are sometimes inflamed with hatred of them, and thus initiate a path back to virtue, for they strive to be unlike those they hate. "For only the divine nature is such that to it even evils are good, since by suitable use of them God draws out as a result some good".[12]

If God is in no way responsible for moral evil, He does nevertheless allow it to happen. St Gregory the Great even goes so far as to say, according to the witness of the book of Job—and this is precisely one of the great lessons of that inspired book—that providence allows the temptations of the devil in view of a greater good (here, the perfection of the holy man): "Satan has a strong desire to tempt the holy man, yet he tells God that *he* should reach out; we must clearly realise, then, that even Satan does not bestow on himself the power to strike, even though his pride against the creator of the universe singles him out. He knows very well that he has no power to do anything on his own, for his very existence as a spirit is not his own doing".[13]

It remains that the human intellect finds itself engulfed in obscurity when it seeks to understand the reasons for which God allows certain things to happen. No created intelligence, unless it enjoys the beatific vision, can grasp the manner in which the freedom of man and the providence of God are harmonised. "It would be to see how infinite justice, infinite mercy and sovereign liberty are identical, without destroying each other, in

---

[12] Boethius, *The Consolation of Philosophy*, IV, 6, LOEB, 1978, p. 371.
[13] St Gregory the Great, *Moral Reflections on the Book of Job*, Vol. 1, Book II, X, 16, translation by Brian Kerns, O.C.S.O., Liturgical Press 2015, p. 132.

the eminence of the Deity, in the intimate love of God, in the inaccessible light where God dwells (1 Tm 6:16), the light which is too strong for our weak eyes and which for us is dark".[14]

Finally, let us evoke the words, at first sight paradoxical, with which St Thomas shows that, far from proving the non-existence of God, evil actually tends to establish it: "If evil exists, God exists. For, there would be no evil if the order of good were taken away, since its privation is evil. But this order would not exist if there were no God".[15] This is another one of those simple truths that our apparently sophisticated world has lost sight of, but which remains rigorously true: we would not even be able to detect evil, or give it a name, if there were no good, no absolute good, which is the measure of the goodness of all creatures.

It is precisely because He is infinite goodness—"His nature is goodness," as St Leo says so expressively in a homily for Christmas[16]—that God makes evil concur to the realisation of good, as St Augustine said above and which it is good to read again here: "For almighty God…, because He is supremely good, would never allow any evil whatsoever to exist in His works if He were not so all-powerful and good as to cause good to emerge from evil itself." There are few truths of our faith that are more consoling than that one.

We now see, even if we do not fully understand, that God can make use of the sins of His creatures to further the good of the universe. But what about that other reality we refer to as "chance"? If God looks after all the details of the universe, how can we explain chance which, by definition, is an event which escapes the order of things and the previsions of reason?

---

[14] R. Garrigou-Lagrange, article "Providence" in *Dictionnaire de Théologie Catholique*. Translation mine.
[15] St Thomas Aquinas, *Summa contra Gentiles*, B. 3, ch. 71.
[16] St Leo the Great, *Sermon 22 on the Nativity*.

It will be good to first recall an obvious fact, namely that "chance" can only exist with regard to an established order. If we perceive unexpected and inexplicable events, it is because there is a pre-existing order in the world, into which such events do not seem to fit, at least as far as our limited knowledge allows us to discern.

"Chance," writes Garrigou-Lagrange in the already cited article on Providence, "is only the accidental encounter of two actions which are not accidental, but intentional, at least in the sense of an unconscious natural inclination, like gravity which is ordered to the cohesion of the universe. Therefore, to say that chance is the first cause of the order of the world, is to explain what is essential by what is accidental, what is primordial by what is accessory; it is to destroy the essential, the natural, all nature and every natural law. There would only be chance meetings, without anything to meet; it is absurd".[17]

This thought is of vital importance. It demonstrates first of all that it is absurd to postulate that things came to be by chance, and secondly that if that were the case, then there is no meaning whatsoever to the universe, in which case no rational discourse or science at all is possible. This means that I could not be writing this book and that you could not be reading it. It explains why it is that when self-styled atheists declare that the universe evolved by chance, they are by the very fact disqualifying their own discourse which pretends to be rational, when, on their own admission, there can be no rationality in the universe to begin with.

The fact of the matter is that there is no such thing as chance. When we use the word, it is only from our point of view, because we do not know the causes of certain happenings. We cannot insist too much on this point. As the Angelic Doctor remarks,

---

[17] R. Garrigou-Lagrange, op. cit.

the constant order of things manifests with the greatest clarity that the world is governed by an excellent being.[18] When you enter a well ordered house, you perceive through this order the directive idea of the master of the house. This conviction is strengthened by the fact that among the beings contained in the universe, the greater majority are irrational beings. If an arrow is guided towards a target, it is because it was shot by an archer who aimed it. If the marvellous little world of the beehive exists to make honey, who designed it? It was clearly foreseen and designed by the architect of the world. The order established in the world of irrational creatures proves enough by itself that there is a creative intelligence, what some modern thinkers have termed an "intelligent design".

Let's come then to an *objection*. "Nothing foreseen can happen by chance. If then everything was foreseen by God, nothing would happen by chance. And thus chance and luck would disappear, which is against common opinion".[19] To *answer*, Thomas has recourse to the distinction between universal and particular cause. From the point of view of the latter, there are things which seem accidental, but from the point of view of the former, even what seems accidental enters into higher plans. The practical scenario St Thomas presents to enlighten this question is that of the apparently chance meeting of two servants, both of whom, unbeknownst to each other, are sent by their master to the same place. From their perspective (what Thomas calls the "particular cause" of the event) the meeting takes place by chance. But from that of the master (what Thomas calls the "universal cause" of the event), it is no chance at all; he had foreseen it, and had a specific goal in mind, even though neither of the servants were aware, and

---

[18] Cf. St Thomas Aquinas, *Summa Theologiae*, Ia q. 103, a. 1.
[19] St Thomas Aquinas, *Summa Theologiae*, Ia, q. 22, a. 2, obj. 1.

possibly never will be. This simple example explains well why it is that we need to remind ourselves that here on earth our perspective does not allow us to see the wider picture. We could also evoke the example of the military leader who is on a mountain and who sees with clarity the approaching conflict in the valley below, in function of which he may give orders that seem unadvised by those who are on the terrain. Those who are there are ignorant of what is to happen, but not the leader from his lofty perspective.

Consequently, what we call "chance" is situated with regard to us, who cannot see from our position in what manner certain events (such as an earthquake or a car accident) enter into the universal plan. There are intersecting lines of causality which are hard, if not impossible, to predict. In his treatise on the virtue of prudence,[20] St Thomas mentions a little known virtue which is annexed to prudence, called by its Greek name *gnome*. *Gnome* helps prudence make a sound judgment in exceptionally difficult cases which do not fall under the common law. What interests us here is the explanation he gives for why this special virtue is required. Sometimes, he explains, things which do not fit into minor principles or ordinances can be reduced to a higher order of things. He specifically mentions the "monstrous births of animals" which is not something that the active seminal force of nature produces normally, and yet, he says, they fall under a higher principle, that of Divine Providence. St Thomas concludes his thought with this phrase: "Hence by considering the active seminal force one could not pronounce a sure judgment on such monstrosities, and yet this is possible if we consider Divine Providence".[21] The wisdom of this reply cannot be overestimated. So many things surpass

---

[20] Cf. St Thomas Aquinas, *Summa Theologiae*, IIa-IIae, q. 47-56.
[21] St Thomas Aquinas, *Summa Theologiae*, IIa-IIae, q. 51, a. 4, corpus.

our capacity to understand, and yet it is not for this reason that they are to be rejected as incompatible with our true good. In passing, it is worth noting that by cultivating the virtue of prudence, one learns how to accept God's providence and to become provident oneself for others.

To put it more simply, and somewhat bluntly: even though our minds must strive to understand as much about God as we can, we must not try to put God into our tiny heads; doing so can lead, at best, to much confusion, and at worst, to insanity. I once met a scientist who unashamedly assured me that the universe is too complex to have been created by anyone. Yes, he actually said it. Such profound arrogance leaves one speechless. What it means ultimately is this: if I can't understand it, it cannot be. The mind is bewildered to encounter such profound stupidity, a bitter fruit of unbridled pride. But sadly it exists.

We can add to this what St Thomas does not say, but which, I think, completes it: if it is true, as was stated earlier, that the universal cause has control over all that escapes the particular cause, it is also true that "chance" must be considered more from the point of view of the proximate cause, than from that of the universal and primary cause. In effect, the Creator having given to the different degrees of beings their particular qualities, He does not intervene habitually in order to change their evolution in history. Certain atmospheric conditions in North America, for example, produce frequent tornadoes. All this was foreseen by Divine Providence. Nevertheless, one cannot say that each time a tornado devastates the American plains, there is a direct intervention of God. This being said, given that even the minute details of beings are dependent upon the omnipotence of the primary cause, we can affirm that this omnipotence is fully engaged in ways which are hidden from us. God sometimes permits catastrophes for a higher end: "Everything which happens in the corporeal creature redounds to the usefulness of man. Earthquakes and other such terrible things are useful in that men, being terrified, may desist from their sins, and so he says: 'hast thou shaken the ungodly out of it?'[22] He speaks here using the comparison of a man who shakes a garment to shake dust or a moth out of it. So also God seems to shake the earth to shake sinners out of it, sometimes by death, sometimes by the amendment of their lives".[23]

Modern man often thinks that, due to his better knowledge of nature, he can explain better the phenomena. Let's say he can often *describe* them better, but not *explain* them better. To explain them, he would need to have a full grasp of all things, and for this he would also have to have the foundations of a good philosophy of nature, which is most often not even considered nowadays. It is indeed one of the sad phenomena of human history that the development of natural empirical sciences went hand in hand with a loss of sound philosophy. What's more, one would also need to have a full knowledge of the entirety of history which no one has but God. At the end of time, God will explain all things to us. Let's learn to wait for Him.

We can go further, however, and say with St Thomas that it would be contrary to the providence of God that everything be the fruit of necessity and that nothing be the fruit of "chance". As proof of this affirmation, he recalls that the perfection of the universe demands beings subject to corruption and to failure. Now, whoever says corruptible says "chance", since chance is born of the ceasing of a cause in its movement towards its end.[24] This principle, which is well explained by the phrase *corruptio unius est generatio alterius*—*the corruption of one*

---

[22] Cf. Job 38:13.
[23] St Thomas Aquinas, *Commentary on the Book of Job*, 38, 2. Translation by Brian Mulladay, slightly adapted.
[24] Cf. St Thomas Aquinas, *Summa contra Gentiles*, B. 3, ch. 74.

is the generation of another,[25] finds a particular application in what concerns man who, as a rational being gifted with free will, achieves his end in his own personal way. If God kept man from erring and provoking disasters, then man would not be free, he would not act in a way which is in conformity with his nature, and he would not attain to his destiny. The marvel of Divine Providence lies precisely in this: God has the capacity to make any failures turn to the good of men. For example, through the correction of punishment, He can procure the good of justice, for the punishment incites others to amend their lives or increase their merits through suffering. The unfair treatment received by the saints only served to give them a greater crown of glory.[26] God knows in advance the moral failures of free creatures, and He turns even these to the good of those who seek Him, just as He turned the malice of the Chief Priests against the Lord Jesus into the Redemption of the human race.

Whoever says free will, then, says possibility of sin. And whoever says possibility of sin, says possible refusal of God and separation from Him. And this brings us to another point, indispensable for a proper understanding of Divine Providence. One of the most fundamental teachings of Divine Revelation, in both the Old and New Testaments, is that God's justice will set all records straight, and it is only in the light of His eternal retribution that many of the evils of this life can be understood. When God allows the triumph of evil over good, He reserves for Himself to punish the unrepentant sinner, just as He reserves to Himself to reward the saints. The awful crimes of history will be set right on the Last Day when the unrepentant evil-doers will be definitively excluded from the

---

[25] Cf. St Thomas Aquinas, *1 Sent*. d. 39, q. 2, a. 2.
[26] Cf. St Thomas Aquinas, *1 Sent*. d. 39, q. 2, a. 2, corpus.

Kingdom of God and those who suffered for His love will be publicly and eternally triumphant. Such is a truth that is all too obvious for anyone who reads Holy Scripture and Sacred Tradition with an open mind.

But perhaps this is precisely one of the reasons for which some people do not see the hand of God at work in the world. St Thomas explains that man sees divine things through the spectacles of his own life: "Divine things are revealed to men in various ways, according as they are variously disposed. For, those who have minds well disposed, perceive divine things rightly, whereas those not so disposed perceive them with a certain confusion of doubt or error: 'for, the sensual man perceiveth not those things that are of the Spirit of God' ".[27] Without belief in an eternal retribution, there is only this life in which to seek justice. But we all know that this is rarely obtained. And so from realising the impossibility of justice in this life to the denying of Divine Providence, there is, without the faith, only one step. The faith is a whole. If one part is denied, the whole edifice falls.

These thoughts on free will were necessary to give as complete a view as possible of the delicate problem of evil and chance. It is also due to his free will that man is one of God's helpers, inasmuch as he is a secondary cause in the full sense of the term, as we saw in the preceding chapter. This brings us to the climax of this study, namely the noble role of secondary causes in the progress of the universe, in particular through that most potent instrument called prayer.

---

[27] St Thomas Aquinas, *Summa Theologiae*, IIIa, q. 55, a. 4, corpus.

4
Providence and Prayer

He will do the will of them that fear Him: and He will hear their prayer, and save them.[1]

IF RATIONAL CREATURES, angels and men, are providence for themselves and for others, among the many forms which this providential activity can take, there is an eminent form called prayer. This is not the place for a complete exposé on the theology of prayer. Our goal is simply to show how prayer is truly a privileged manner for contributing to the proper and good functioning of the world towards eternal beatitude. As one eminent contemporary Thomist remarks: "One of the decisive criteria for appreciating the truth of a theory on providence is its aptitude for giving prayer its proper place in the divine government".[2]

We might begin by mentioning the three errors about prayer which St Thomas takes issue with in his own teaching on the subject.[3] The first error can be formulated this way.

---

[1] Ps 144:19.
[2] Serge-Thomas Bonino, O.P., in "Providence et causes secondes, l'exemple de la prière", in *Cahiers d'histoire de la philosophie: Saint Thomas d'Aquin*, Le Cerf, 2010, p. 501. Translation mine.
[3] Saint Thomas treats this question in at least four different parts of his writings: *Summa contra gentiles*, l. 3, c. 96; *Super librum Dionysii: De divinis nominibus*, c. 3; *Lectura super Matthaeum*, c. 6; *Summa theologiae*, IIa-IIae, q. 83, a. 2.

Human affairs are in no way within the realm of providence; consequently, prayer is perfectly useless. In other words, God does not care about what happens in this world, so don't bother asking Him for help. This is the approach taken by various systems of thought for which God did indeed create the world, but leaves it to its own devices. It is pretty much the Aristotelian or Deist approach to God, the Prime Mover who sets everything in motion, and then goes off and forgets it. This theory actually synthesises two ancient errors: that of the Epicureans who quite simply denied providence and attributed everything to chance; and that of certain Aristotelians who attributed to God only a general providence over things which does not enter into the details of individual life.

The second error affirms that God's providence is indeed concerned with men, but its designs are immutable, and so it is not worth praying for anything, for either something has been decreed by God and will happen of necessity, or it has not and nothing will be able to make it happen. This error, called determinism, is found in various forms depending on the perspective from which one is approaching it. Theologically, such determinism is founded on a false conception of divine immutability. In an overly simplistic way, it deduces falsely from the fact that God is immutable and immobile the conclusion that things cannot change in this world either, since an immutable God created it. Cosmologically, this determinism is quite simply astral. That is to say, everything that happens on earth is determined by the position of the stars and planets; there is nothing really that we can do to change things, for we ourselves are within a universe dominated by the cosmos. In other words, just as the ocean ebb and flow is determined by the phases of the moon, so the fluctuations of human wills can be influenced (though not imposed) by the moon and the stars. Does not the expression "lunatic" take its origin from the conviction (still prevalent today) that the strange activities of certain individuals are caused at least to a certain extent by the moon? Finally, from the perspective of what we might call a belief in destiny, determinism believes that, due to an unbreakable chain of causes, the destiny of each individual, even in its most minute details, is already established, and we are only, as involved spectators, watching the playing out of what has been decreed at some mysterious higher level. St Augustine, having been entangled in it for some time himself, speaks at length of this approach in his *Confessions*.[4]

What is of particular interest to us here is that these first two groups, even though they approach the question from very different perspectives, both arrive at the same conclusion: prayer is useless. Either God does not care what happens to you and you will not induce Him to take interest, or your future is already set in stone and there is nothing you can do to change it. So don't pray, because it won't help, and could possibly even nurture in you the illusion that you can actually make things better by doing so.

The third error takes a very different, actually, the opposite, approach. Here, prayer is deemed useful. It is actually so useful that it can cause God to change His plans.[5] From this perspective, prayer is seen as a kind of bargain, or worse, a struggle with God, in which the one who prays seeks to make God change His mind when He had already decided to do otherwise. Some passages of the Bible, it is true, seem to favour this concept of prayer. For example, it is said that God repented and went back on His decision concerning the death of King Ezechias (or Hezekiah).[6] Or in the book of Jonah, God changes His mind and does not punish the Ninevites as He

---

[4] See for example, Book 7, ch. 6.
[5] Cf. St Thomas Aquinas, *Summa Theologiae*, IIa-IIae, q. 83, a. 2.
[6] Cf. Is 38.

had said He would.[7] Or again, there is the episode of Jacob's wrestling with the angel at the crossing of Jabok in which he prevails over God.[8]

Regarding this third error, Aquinas keenly points out the great difference between asking something of a man and asking something of God. When one beseeches a man, one wants him to take into consideration a situation he is ignorant of, in order to inflect his will. With God, it cannot be so, for He is ignorant of nothing that concerns men: *Your heavenly Father knows what you need;*[9] as for His will, it is immutable. Since this third error is actually based on what it deems to be ignorance in God and also on His supposed changeability, it holds no water, for God is omniscient and immutable.

Commenting on the Lord's Prayer in his lecture on the Gospel of St Matthew, St Thomas notes that the very first words of this prayer are enough to discard the three aforementioned errors. He points out that when we say *Our Father who art in heaven*, we are professing God's paternity, and like every Father he provides for the future, and is therefore provident. Aquinas quotes here a very consoling passage of the Book of Wisdom in which the inspired author turns his gaze to the way in which God guides a voyage through the raging waves of the sea : "But Thy providence, O Father, governeth: for Thou hast made a way even in the sea, and a most sure path among the waves, showing that Thou art able to save out of all things, yea though a man went to sea without art".[10] In the same way, when one speaks of a father it is with regard to a son, and when one speaks of a lord it is with regard to a servant... But,

---
[7] Cf. Jonah 3:10.
[8] Cf. Gen 32:25-29.
[9] Mt 6:32.
[10] Wis 14:1-4.

being a son means being free. It is therefore not imposed upon as a constraint. When we say *who art in Heaven*, we profess that God does not change. Prayer therefore aims at believing that God disposes all things in a way that is becoming of their nature. God is immutable, but man is submitted to change. Therefore God's providence wants man to attain his end by his mutable actions. Thus, the proper expression is neither that prayer changes providence or that it escapes from it, but that it is submitted to it and cooperates with it.[11]

But how can we admit, on one hand, that God has an eternal plan that does not change, and, on the other, that He lets himself be moved by the prayer of His creatures? The response brings into play one of the principles already evoked concerning the manner of action of secondary causes. Indeed, prayer does not change the eternal order of things, the way in which God governs the creatures He has made. All creatures, indeed, exist under the very order of things. Now, there is nothing to prevent God from allowing that in response to prayer some contingent order of His Providence be changed; on the contrary, all the inferior causes are contained under the order of God and can be changed by Him. When this happens, Holy Scripture uses expressions such as: God turned around, God repented, God did not do as He had decreed, etc. It is not His eternal disposition that is changed, but some effect of those dispositions. St Gregory actually says: "Even if almighty God does often change a decision, He never changes His judgment".[12] He is said to repent, metaphorically speaking, in the sense that He is disposed like one who repents, for whom it is

---

[11] Cf. St Thomas Aquinas, *Lecture on the Gospel of Matthew*, c. 6.
[12] St Gregory the Great, *Moral Reflections on the Book of Job*, Vol. 3, Book XVI, x, 14, translation by Brian Kerns, O.C.S.O., Liturgical Press 2016, p. 273.

proper to change what he had been doing. In the same way, He is said metaphorically to become angry, in the sense that, by punishing, He produces the same effect as an angry person.[13]

We might go further and preclude another objection by saying that when we pray for things which may seem contrary to what would ordinarily happen, we actually offer worship to God and His providence in the sense that we recognise in this way our dependence upon the manner in which God governs our lives and the world. Even more can we say that, by means of prayer that is humble, confident and persevering, we cooperate with God in governing the world, for He has from all eternity decided that such and such salutary effect would not happen without our prayer and intercession. God likes us to "force His hand" as the parable of the wicked judge bears witness:

> "There was a certain widow in that city; and she came to him, saying: Avenge me of my adversary. And he would not for a long time. But afterwards he said within himself: Although I fear not God nor regard man, yet because this widow is troublesome to me, I will avenge her, lest continually coming she weary me. And the Lord said: Hear what the unjust judge saith. And will not God revenge his elect who cry to him day and night? And will he have patience in their regard?"[14]

Or again, that of the importunate friend:

> "And he said to them: Which of you shall have a friend and shall go to him at midnight and shall say to him: Friend, lend me three loaves, because a friend of

---

[13] Cf. St Thomas Aquinas, *Summa contra Gentiles*, B. 3, ch. 96.
[14] Lk 18:3-7.

mine is come off his journey to me and I have not what to set before him. And he from within should answer and say: Trouble me not; the door is now shut, and my children are with me in bed. I cannot rise and give thee. Yet if he shall continue knocking, I say to you, although he will not rise and give him because he is his friend; yet, because of his importunity, he will rise and give him as many as he needeth. And I say to you: Ask, and it shall be given you: seek, and you shall find: knock, and it shall be opened to you. For every one that asketh receiveth: and he that seeketh findeth: and to him that knocketh it shall be opened".[15]

If we were to ask why God wants to associate men with His providential designs, giving them to merit in some way by prayer the gifts He offers, the response is obvious according to the principles exposed above concerning secondary causes in general: God wants to give to each the dignity of cooperating in obtaining our ultimate destiny, for ourselves and for others. We truly are co-workers with Divine Providence. We can, however, number two other decisive reasons for this.

The first concerns the harmony and solidarity that exists, or should exist, between men. By praying for another person, one cannot but feel involved in their destiny. What happens to my brother or my sister concerns me, for we are one and the same body. In this way, prayer leads the unity of the Church to its perfection. "We ought to desire good things not only for ourselves, but also for others: for this is essential to the love which we owe to our neighbour.... Therefore charity requires us to pray for others".[16]

---

[15] Lk 11:5-10.
[16] St Thomas Aquinas, *Summa Theologiae*, IIa-IIae, q. 83, a. 7, corpus.

The second is for us personally. When we pray, it is not God that we change, but ourselves. By formulating our requests, even if only in our mind, we are already committing ourselves in some way to wanting what we are asking for, and we thus obtain the capacity to receive it from God. "Prayer, then, for obtaining something from God is necessary for man on account of the very one who prays, that he may reflect on his shortcomings and may turn his mind to desiring fervently and piously what he hopes to gain by his petition. In this way he is rendered fit to receive the favour".[17]

It is in this sense that St Thomas affirms that prayer *expresses the desire* (*explicativa desiderii*),[18] and is *the unfolding of our will to God* (*explicatio propriae voluntatis apud Deum*),[19] *a certain unfolding of our desires* (*quaedam desideriorum explicatio*).[20] The action implied by the Latin word which St Thomas employs in all three of these expressions is literally the action of unrolling, unfolding. Prayer unfolds our desires, it unrolls before God what we would like to see happen, it is the expression of what we want. By prayer, we make ourselves, as it were, to develop, to explain, all our desires, vividly conscious of our needs and our powerlessness to pull ourselves through on our own. In this way, the desire increases, goaded on, as it were, stoked up by the thought that God gives us what we ask for.

In this way, it becomes clear that the one who prays does not remain passive, but takes the initiative. Under the influence of prevenient grace, he goes out to meet God and becomes thus an actor in his own sanctification. Since this prayer bursts forth, as it were, from the grace of God, it increases in us the desire to

---

[17] St Thomas Aquinas, *Compendium Theologiae*, l. 2, c. 2.
[18] Cf. St Thomas Aquinas, *Summa Theologiae*, IIa-IIae, q. 83, a. 14, obj. 2.
[19] Cf. St Thomas Aquinas, *Summa Theologiae*, IIIa, q. 21, a. 1, corpus.
[20] Cf. St Thomas Aquinas, *Super Epistolam ad Romanos*, c. 8, l. 5.

receive precisely what God wants to give us, and it thus takes on an infallible effectiveness. This goes for everything that regards the obtaining of eternal salvation. St Augustine had eloquently spoken of this desire which increases by attentiveness and persevering prayer: "Their desire is delayed, in order that it may increase; it increases, in order that it may receive. For it is not any little thing that God will give to him who desires, nor does he need to be little exercised to be made fit to receive so great a good: not anything which He hath made will God give, but Himself who made all things. Exercise thyself to receive God: that which their shalt have for ever, desire thou for along time…".[21]

Following Augustine, Aquinas thinks that this is what Our Lord was alluding to when He said: "If you ask me anything in my name, I will do it".[22] "How could he say, *Whatever you ask I will do it,* since we see that His faithful ask and do not receive? According to Augustine, we should consider here that he first says, *in my name*, and then adds, *I will do it.* The name of Christ is the name of salvation: *You shall call His name Jesus, for He will save His people from their sins.*[23] Therefore, one who asks for something pertaining to salvation asks in the name of Christ".[24]

This does not in any way mean that we are forbidden from asking for temporal favours. A man in the state of grace is capable, under the motion of the Holy Spirit, of discerning what is really good for himself. He can and should ask the Lord for certain particular goods, even material and temporal ones. Nevertheless, this request should always be conditional. The

---

[21] St Augustine, *Commentary on Psalm 83*, 3. Oxford translation.
[22] Jn 14:14.
[23] Mt 1:21.
[24] St Thomas Aquinas, *Lecture on the Gospel of John*, ch. 14, 3. Translation by Fabian R. Larcher, O.P.

secondary cause remains a secondary cause, and Divine Providence sees further than we do. Since it knows better than we do what we really need, we mustn't be surprised if our prayers are not answered in the way we were hoping for. For if God refuses such and such a grace, it is to give us a greater grace which will be more useful to us.

Another reason for which our prayer is not heard can be found in a lack of perseverance or a lack of fervour in asking. Once again the Angelic Doctor comes to our aid, making a comparison with natural realities.[25] If one puts an object in motion, if one wants it to reach its destiny, the movement must be carried through to completion. In the same way, if one desires to obtain a grace from God, it is not enough to pray for it once. One must be insistent. Otherwise the expected result will not ensue. This is why the Lord says that "we ought always to pray and not to faint";[26] in the same way the Apostle commands: "Pray without ceasing".[27] Furthermore, the nearness of the soul to God moves Him to hear the prayer of that soul; now, one becomes near to Him through contemplation, devout affection, and humble but firm intention. If we do not approach God in this way, we are not capable of being heard by Him. Hence, it is said in the Psalm: 'He has had regard to the prayer of the humble';[28] and in St James: "Let him ask in faith, nothing wavering".[29]

There is more. Taking inspiration from St Paul's expression: "we are God's helpers",[30] St Thomas goes so far as to say that *our prayer helps God* in some way. What does he mean by this?

---

[25] Cf. St Thomas Aquinas, *Summa contra Gentiles*, B. 3, ch. 96.
[26] Lk 18:1.
[27] 1 Thessalonians 5:17.
[28] Psalm 101:18.
[29] James 1:6.
[30] 1 Cor 3:9.

He does *not* mean to say that God is weak and needs our help, but rather that it is the sovereign will of the Master to make use of us as helpers. This marvel of divine condescension is in no way due to any deficiency on God's side, but always, as we have already pointed out several times, from his desire to endow His creatures and lift them to the rank of cooperators in the divine work.[31] And so in this way it becomes clear that "the relation between Divine Providence and human freedom is not one of antithesis, but of communion in love".[32]

Now, this role, before being that of every believer, belongs eminently to the humanity of Christ. Aquinas explains one of the principal reasons for which God wanted to assume this living instrument in the unique person of the Word when He could simply have cancelled our debt and given us eternal life out of pure mercy. It is more noble and more glorious, he says, to merit something than to simply received it gratuitously. This is made clear by the fact that to be the cause of oneself is more noble than to be caused by another. Speaking absolutely, as we saw earlier, God causes all things, but He also gives creatures, especially rational creatures, to be real and true causes. By co-operating with God and His grace, one can truly merit further grace, and this is by far more noble than to receive it without merit. And so it is better to have a thing by merit than to have it without merit.[33]

If Aquinas considers God in His reality of self-subsistent being, he sees at the same time that it is this reality which gives existence and value to human freedom. It is precisely because Father, Son and Holy Spirit are infinitely, incommensurably Being, Truth, and loving Goodness, that They can give creatures to be good themselves and play a role in salvation. For

---

[31] Cf. St Thomas Aquinas, *Summa Theologiae*, Ia, q. 23, a. 8, ad 2.
[32] St John Paul II, *General Audience*, 30 April 1986. Translation mine.
[33] Cf. St Thomas Aquinas, *Summa Theologiae*, IIIa, q. 19, a. 3.

intellectual creatures, that implies true freedom and real autonomy, even if it remains relative. While many do not grasp how we can still be free even if God is the cause of all things, Thomas affirms that such a confusion comes from the fact that one imagines God and creatures acting as univocal causes. In reality, God is so infinitely powerful and good that He creates and supports the freedom of His creatures. In His infinite transcendence, God causes, and the creature causes, the same effect, albeit in another order. God gives spiritual creatures to be free causes. And this doctrine has important and very practical effects on our spiritual life, on the way we consider God, His providence, our activity and our prayer.

> "One striking teaching in Thomas is his view of God as self-subsisting act of being with regard to the reality and worth of human existence and freedom. For him, precisely because the Father, Son and Holy Spirit are so *infinitely*, un-measurably Being, Truth, and Loving-Goodness, They can and do allow created reality a full role in history. This role is wisely and lovingly guided by Them, but it is real. For intellectual creatures this means real freedom and real if relative autonomy. Many are puzzled as to how God can cause everything and yet we can be free. Thomas would say that this puzzlement comes because they imagine God and ourselves to be in the same order of being, to act as univocal causes. Thomas says simply that God is so *infinitely* powerful and good that He creates and sustains our very freedom! It is not as if God has trillions of trillion ergs of energy and our free act takes away one erg from His, so that God's glory is lessened by that much. No, in His infinite transcendence God causes, and we in our created order

cause the one effect, God enabling us to be causes and to be free causes. This may seem very speculative and mysterious, but it is most practical for spirituality, for how one views God and His providence, our activity, and our prayer".[34]

If this availability of God in our regard is founded on His own goodness, it is equally founded on the demands of true friendship, which God has so mercifully initiated with us: "You are my friends, if you do the things that I command you. I will not now call you servants: for the servant knoweth not what his lord doth. But I have called you friends. because all things, whatsoever I have heard of my Father, I have made known to you".[35] It pertains precisely to the essence of friendship that the lover want the fulfilment of the desire of the one he loves, for he wishes all that is good and perfect for the beloved.[36]

Among the saints, one could cite numerous examples of souls who understood this truth so clearly that they could only respond to such astounding love by total surrender of their lives. St Therese of Lisieux is a luminous example who continues to inspire many souls. She became a Carmelite at a very young age in order to save souls through prayer and penance. Coming to fully realise the extent to which she was loved by God and had become one of His friends, she wanted to share that conviction with others. In so doing, she became mother and providence for a multitude of souls, for she acted

---

[34] W. H. Principe, O.S.B., "Thomas Aquinas' Spirituality," in *The Etienne Gilson Series 7*, Pontifical Institute of Mediaeval Studies (1984) 19-20. Translation mine.

[35] Jn 15:14-15.

[36] Cf. St Thomas Aquinas, *Summa contra Gentiles*, B. 3, ch. 95.

in a most wise and provident way. Having become providence for souls, she is truly, in imitation of the Mother of God, *virgo prudentissima*.

Finally, far from taking anything away from God, prayer glorifies Him fully, for it establishes His providence. By prayer, men "let God know of" their needs, and God, by answering their prayers, gives them to be fruitful. But if there is no providence, then prayer obtains nothing, for God would then know nothing of human affairs.[37] Prayer is an integral part of the realisation of Divine Providence.

We can find no better conclusion to this chapter than this passage from the book of Apocalypse in which the joint activity of angels and men in their prayer to God is emphasised. Prayers of the saints, incense of the angel, united in the same offering before the throne of God for the world: such are the secondary causes, the co-workers of Divine Providence, at work in all their glory and dignity:

"Another angel came and stood before the altar, having a golden censer: and there was given to him much incense, that he should offer of the prayers of all saints, upon the golden altar which is before the throne of God. And the smoke of the incense of the prayers of the saints ascended up before God from the hand of the angel".[38]

---

[37] Cf. St Thomas Aquinas, *Commentary on the Book on Job*, 5, 2.
[38] Apoc 8:3-4.

Conclusion
Providence and Hope

It brings much pleasure to have knowledge of all the things in the world; and therefore it is supereminently pleasurable to see the dispositions of Divine Providence.[1]

THE DOGMA OF Divine Providence is one of the most consoling of our Christian faith. Through it we know that Someone thought of us from all eternity, that He is keeping watch over us at every moment; nothing escapes Him; He orders absolutely all things, for the good of His elect. This doctrine is most profitable for reviving within us and helping us cultivate the virtue of hope. Thanks to this theological virtue, we know that by relying on the divine omnipotence which wants our good, we will attain to the eternal kingdom. "Providence is as a constant and unceasing confirmation of the work of creation in all its richness and variety. It signifies the constant and uninterrupted presence of God as creator, in all creation: a presence which creates continually and reaches continually the deepest roots of all that exists, to work there as primary cause of being and action".[2]

This virtue of hope will also give us greater assurance to assume with courage and boldness the various responsibilities that might be laid upon us. God loves us and esteems us to

---

[1] St Thomas Aquinas, *Commentary on Psalm 26*.
[2] St John Paul II, *General Audience,* 7 May 1986. Translation mine.

the point of making us His collaborators in the work of the salvation of souls. As we strive to spread His kingdom on earth, we know that we are only instruments and co-workers. If God associates us with His work, it is truly He who is at work in His Son Jesus Christ:

> "God alone, beyond any intermediary, makes Himself present to the human person whom He alone created and predestined. The instruments which He created and used, can only disappear before the One who holds in His hands the entire universe, all of History, and each one of us. Nevertheless, where the power of our action ceases, we can still have our place, and God wants it. Here it is no longer a matter of acting, and one is no longer, strictly speaking, an instrument. One must pray. To pray is, I make bold to say, to act upon God to obtain from Him that His providence intervene. This would be impossible and incomprehensible if it were not understood that it is divine grace alone which inspires in us such a desire. It is Jesus Christ who inspires our prayer".[3]

When we become aware of this marvellous doctrine, we then understand that we have no excuse for not playing our role, our providential role in the history of the world. Instead of demanding that God give us an account, or losing our time in futile inquisitions into the mysterious workings of His Providence, we will do better to pray. The next time we are shocked by some catastrophe that hits impoverished populations, or when our own fate seems so unfair, instead of complaining and doubting, let us have recourse to that most powerful lever

---

[3] M.-J. Nicolas, *Croire en la providence?* Pierre Téqui (1995) 100.

we have with which we can lift up the world: prayer. In those times, when we do not feel like praying, let us use a bit of violence over ourselves and remember that "the kingdom of heaven suffereth violence, and the violent bear it away".[4] Prayer changes the pray-er (the one who prays); prayer changes the world; prayer is the privileged manner of working together with God to provide all good things.

May the Mother of Holy Hope, Mary Immaculate, help us to lift up our eyes to Heaven with confidence renewed in the ineffable dispositions of Divine Providence; may she obtain for us a divinely founded and growing assurance that we have a role to play, subordinate but essential, in history, and in particular in that part of history which is the salvation of souls.

> *O God, whose providence in the ordering of all things never fails; we humbly beseech Thee to put away from us all that is harmful, and to give us all that is profitable for us.*
>
> *Missale Romanum, Seventh Sunday after Pentecost*

---

[4] Mt 11:12.

Appendix

Catechism of the Catholic Church
Paragraphs 309-314

PROVIDENCE AND THE SCANDAL OF EVIL

309 If God the Father almighty, the Creator of the ordered and good world, cares for all his creatures, why does evil exist? To this question, as pressing as it is unavoidable and as painful as it is mysterious, no quick answer will suffice. Only Christian faith as a whole constitutes the answer to this question: the goodness of creation, the drama of sin and the patient love of God who comes to meet man by his covenants, the redemptive Incarnation of his Son, his gift of the Spirit, his gathering of the Church, the power of the sacraments and his call to a blessed life to which free creatures are invited to consent in advance, but from which, by a terrible mystery, they can also turn away in advance. There is not a single aspect of the Christian message that is not in part an answer to the question of evil.

310 But why did God not create a world so perfect that no evil could exist in it? With infinite power God could always create something better (Cf. St. Thomas Aquinas, *Summa Theologiae* I, 25, 6). But with infinite wisdom and goodness God freely willed to create a world "in a state of journeying" towards its ultimate perfection. In God's plan this process of becoming involves the appearance of certain beings and the disappearance of others, the existence of the more perfect alongside the less perfect, both constructive and destructive forces of nature. With physical good there exists also physical evil as long as creation has not reached perfection (Cf. St. Thomas Aquinas, *Summa Contra Gentiles*, III, 71).

311 Angels and men, as intelligent and free creatures, have to journey toward their ultimate destinies by their free choice and preferential love. They can therefore go astray. Indeed, they have sinned. Thus has moral evil, incommensurably more harmful than physical evil, entered the world. God is in no way, directly or indirectly, the cause of moral evil (Cf. St. Augustine, *De libero arbitrio* I, 1, 2: PL 32, 1221-1223; St. Thomas Aquinas, *Summa Theologiae* I-II, 79, 1). He permits it, however, because he respects the freedom of his creatures and, mysteriously, knows how to derive good from it:

For almighty God…, because he is supremely good, would never allow any evil whatsoever to exist in his works if he were not so all-powerful and good as to cause good to emerge from evil itself (St. Augustine, *Enchiridion* 11, 3: PL 40, 236).

312 In time we can discover that God in his almighty providence can bring a good from the consequences of an evil, even a moral evil, caused by his creatures: "It was not you", said Joseph to his brothers, "who sent me here, but God. . . You meant evil against me; but God meant it for good, to bring it about that many people should be kept alive" (Gen 45:8; 50:20; cf. Tob 2:12, Vulgate).

From the greatest moral evil ever committed—the rejection and murder of God's only Son, caused by the sins of all men—God, by his grace that "abounded all the more" (Cf. Rom 5:20) brought the greatest of goods: the glorification of Christ and our redemption. But for all that, evil never becomes a good.

313 "We know that in everything God works for good for those who love him" (Rom 8:28).

The constant witness of the saints confirms this truth:
St. Catherine of Siena said to "those who are scandalized

and rebel against what happens to them": "Everything comes from love, all is ordained for the salvation of man, God does nothing without this goal in mind." (St. Catherine of Siena, *Dialogue* IV, 138 "On Divine Providence".)

St. Thomas More, shortly before his martyrdom, consoled his daughter: "Nothing can come but that that God wills. And I make me very sure that whatsoever that be, seem it never so bad in sight, it shall indeed be the best." (*The Correspondence of Sir Thomas More*, ed. Elizabeth F. Rogers, Princeton: Princeton University Press, 1947, letter 206, lines 661-663.)

Dame Julian of Norwich: "Here I was taught by the grace of God that I should steadfastly keep me in the faith… and that at the same time I should take my stand on and earnestly believe in what our Lord shewed in this time—that 'all manner [of] thing shall be well.'" (Julian of Norwich, *The Revelations of Divine Love*, tr. James Walshe SJ, London: 1961, ch. 32, 99-100.)

314 We firmly believe that God is master of the world and of its history. But the ways of his providence are often unknown to us. Only at the end, when our partial knowledge ceases, when we see God "face to face", (I Cor 13:12) will we fully know the ways by which—even through the dramas of evil and sin—God has guided his creation to that definitive sabbath rest (cf. Gen 2:2) for which he created heaven and earth.

www.ingramcontent.com/pod-product-compliance
Lightning Source LLC
Chambersburg PA
CBHW030303010526
44107CB00053B/1797